Idea Poetry

To Guide Your Passionate Pursuits

MARIE KORDUS

BALBOA.
PRESS
A DIVISION OF HAY HOUSE

Balboa Press books may be ordered through booksellers or by contacting:

Balboa Press
A Division of Hay House
1663 Liberty Drive
Bloomington, IN 47403
www.balboapress.com
1 (877) 407-4847

Because of the dynamic nature of the Internet, any web addresses or links contained in this book may have changed since publication and may no longer be valid. The views expressed in this work are solely those of the author and do not necessarily reflect the views of the publisher, and the publisher hereby disclaims any responsibility for them.

The author of this book does not dispense medical advice or prescribe the use of any technique as a form of treatment for physical, emotional, or medical problems without the advice of a physician, either directly or indirectly. The intent of the author is only to offer information of a general nature to help you in your quest for emotional and spiritual well-being. In the event you use any of the information in this book for yourself, which is your constitutional right, the author and the publisher assume no responsibility for your actions.

Any people depicted in stock imagery provided by Thinkstock are models, and such images are being used for illustrative purposes only.
Certain stock imagery © Thinkstock.

Print information available on the last page.

ISBN: 978-1-5043-6015-9 (sc)
ISBN: 978-1-5043-6016-6 (hc)
ISBN: 978-1-5043-6026-5 (e)

Library of Congress Control Number: 2016909724

Balboa Press rev. date: 07/05/2016

To Gabby, Squeak, and Zelda, my furry companions, teachers, muses, and guiding geniuses. Until we meet again at the rainbow bridge.

Contents

Preface

This book came about as a way to demonstrate how my unique idea poetry designs can be used as inspiration and encouragement in pursuit of a desired outcome. Words and images are powerful and one look may be exactly what's needed to complete your project or begin a new venture.

I share my process, using idea poetry, for passionately pursuing my own worthy goals and encourage you to use my method. After reading the contents of prose and poetry I suggest you look at all designs and decide which serve you on your current path.

The read is simple to let your imagination, unique set of experiences and current state of mind see what you will in the idea poetry designs and let them work for you.

If one story or one design helps you on your journey to find meaning in your life, to find your gifts, and encourages you to share them it has served its purpose.

Idea Poetry, the book, is from a perspective of someone just like you, someone who had a dream. Every great pursuit begins with a dream and I hope by taking action on mine it inspires you.

Discover who you are, what you want, and what you want to be known for. Leave your best on the stage of your life and you will become the inspiration for someone else.

Acknowledgements

Heartfelt gratitude to: my publisher, Balboa Press, for their guidance; my Passion Project Group: Alison Spielmann, Louise Soper, Nancy Caldwell, Taryn Poole and Nicole Criona for their initial read and support through the process; Elizabeth Henderson and Richard Sturdevant for their story and generational perspective; Lyna Faucett and Sherrie Bang for their insightful comments after reading the manuscript; Will Campbell and Danilo Roque from Quantasy, my Digital Marketing Agency, for their collaboration over the years.

Introduction

I can tell you that I have worked since my teenage years, although I have never had a job. A career, maybe; a calling, absolutely, doing and making work uniquely mine for a life filled with passion, purpose, and possibilities.

Everybody has a purpose; everybody searches to find her own way; everybody needs inspiration to move toward an inspired life of meaning. Someone somewhere is going to begin her journey today. Why not let it be you?

We all have something, a time when we feel alive and in our element. A realization, an ah-ha moment, a shift in perspective, an enlightened instant that tells us this is where we belong. We think, *This is what I am meant to be doing, and by doing this, I can make a difference in the lives of others, fulfill my purpose, and add meaning to my life.*

How do we get there? It's a process, a system, like everything else we do on a daily basis. It's awareness of who we are, what we want, and what feeds our souls and brings joy. It's when fear disappears; it's when the ego steps aside for us to follow our hearts and find peace within. By telling a piece of my story, I can help you find your passions. I have unique tools to offer you to follow your heart and stay the course.

You're probably asking yourself, "What makes her think she can help me find my passions, follow my dreams, and move toward my ideal life?" I asked myself the same question, because I'm just like you, making my way every day. The difference may be that I have examined my path, my struggles, my setbacks, and my triumphs, and I have taken time to write them down. I've noticed common actions attributable to my many journeys that have helped me move forward as I take on new ventures. Through storytelling and my ability to create my unique *Idea Poetry,* as I call it, I will bring life to seven steps, plus one to help you take action on the adventure that is your life.

The story behind the *Idea Poetry* designs is that I created all of them not in any particular order, and not with any intention of having them put together to be a step-by-step guide. In fact I have over thirty inspirational designs, and by selecting different designs and reordering them, they encourage a different path. For our purposes, we are going to concentrate on discovering your passions and taking steps to live your ideal life. All *Idea Poetry* designs are included in a later section of this book.

How *Idea Poetry* Came into Existence

I was a fine arts major in college with a secondary interest in philosophy. However, like most people my life after college took several twists and turns. I eventually found myself in the broadcast industry. I started as a media salesperson, and then I had an extensive period as a sales manager. During this time, I was able to integrate my interest in art and philosophy within my day-to-day work by creating *Idea Poetry*. Selling radio and television time is highly competitive, and in order to keep my sales team motivated, I would create one piece per year. I always tried to reflect the essence of the current time, however they are timeless and meaningful for anyone at any time.

Some of the designs were created in the early 1980s and are still relevant today, and they will continue to be in the years to come. It was a way for me to record my life experiences in a unique way and share them. I started producing them as one-sided cards, and I sent them as Christmas gifts. They were hardly holiday messages, however family, friends, and colleagues looked forward to them. They told me they framed them as wall art or desktop prints to look at during times of personal struggle. That encouraged me and gave me the confidence to do more, and knowing it was anticipated, I wanted to make certain the messages were universal and resonated with people everywhere, not just those who knew me. Over the years, I have been told they never cease to provide that lift, that inner boost; they keep on giving.

As a broadcast sales manager, I also developed a class for new salespeople entering the industry. The content was specifically on new business development, the heart of every sales organization. As the class evolved, I found it was very natural for me to integrate my *Idea Poetry* into the curriculum as gifts at the end of class, or as visuals to emphasize specific steps in my process for new business development. This added another dimension to my sales class by providing tangible, motivational tools people could take with them. I began looking differently at these simple words and images, and I developed several visual programs using different *Idea Poetry* designs. I had all designs made into animated e-cards to add choices for their use. As examples, *New Team Member Welcome* uses seven pieces of idea poetry for managers or team leaders to use as new people join their team. On a personal note, a five-piece program offers inspiration to *Lift Someone's Spirit*. Both programs are portrayed later in the book, as are all *Idea Poetry*. You will have the opportunity to explore possibilities and combinations that work for you.

Seven Steps to Pursue Your Passions, Plus One

1. Passion

The adventure is our passion.

Passion is interest plus a burning desire.

Discover your passion by noticing those moments of flow, absorption, when the time just passes as you are involved in work that is uniquely yours.

This is the foundation of the process, and it begins personally with me, with you.

Go there.

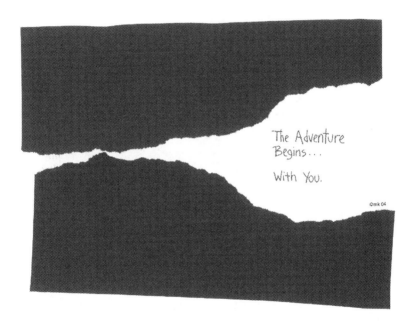

The Adventure
Begins...

With You.

©mk 04

2. Action

Action cures fear, and there is always fear when starting a new venture.

Nothing happens, until something moves and I take that first action step.

Set a goal, make a commitment of the will, and begin to move toward the goal.

If I do nothing, nothing happens.

Begin by taking action.

NOTHING HAPPENS

UNTIL
SOMETHING
MOVES

3. Believe

If I believe I can do something, I can do it. I will do it.
Believe in what you are doing, what you are committed to; believe it from your heart.
Lead with your heart, and your head and hands will follow.
Little steps come together to make the whole.
I believe in you.

4. Focus

I get what I focus on.

Nothing can take the place of a concentrated effort on a single endeavor. Prioritize time every day or every week, whatever your schedule allows for, to work on your pursuit; let nothing interfere with that time.

You get what you focus on.

What will you get?

5. Simplify

Starting a new project always seems overwhelming.
Break it down into manageable steps, chunks, so it doesn't seem so daunting.
Write them down.
Check the list.
I pick up where I left off from the day before.
It's old school.
It works.

SIMPLIFY

6. Persist

Some people say attitude is everything; I say attitude is *almost* everything.
Persistence, sticking with it consistently, is everything.
Obstacles will show up, life events, negative comments from others.
My own mind creating problems, doubt, and worry.
It will happen to you too.
Stay the course; you will succeed beyond expectations.

7. Reflect

Reflection during the process and upon completion of a pursuit is essential for improvement and a positive experience.
I debrief on my own or with someone else.
What worked?
What didn't work?
What could have been done better?
Continual reflection produces the best possible result and inspiration to move forward.

+1. Go For It

After doing the above seven steps, surely I have had success, so it's time to begin again.
A new passionate pursuit, or improve and enhance what was just completed.
It's never over!
Good luck.

GO
FOR
IT

© MK 90

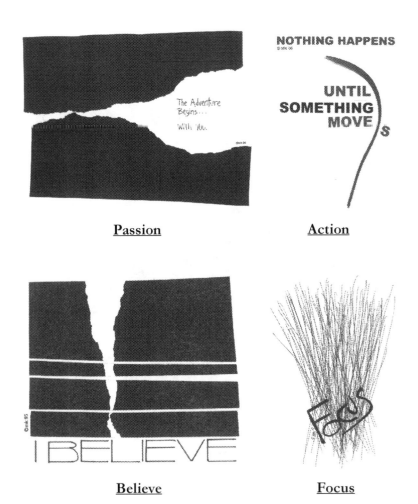

Passion

NOTHING HAPPENS

UNTIL SOMETHING MOVES

Action

I BELIEVE

Believe

Focus

Simplify

Persist

Reflect

Begin Again!

How You Can Use the Steps

You're probably saying, "I know all this stuff," and the truth is you probably do. They are tools, and any one of them can stand alone to help you on your path. Together they are a powerful guide. When practiced in sequential order, they can work for you and keep you on track in your pursuits.

How can you use them? Surround yourself in them; use them as fuel, an inner boost when you need it. Words and images are influential, and just a look or a quick read can provide the inspiration you need to keep motivated after a setback, a discouraging comment, or self-doubt that creeps in during any passionate pursuit. I have a room, my working space, with *Idea Poetry* that is poster size, and my refrigerator and file cabinets have *Idea Poetry* magnets displayed. In my wallet I carry cards, business card size, that serve as consistent, gentle reminders to help keep me on track. I never want to find myself saying, "Now what?"

We've all been there. We read an inspirational quote, go to a motivational seminar, or listen to an inspiring podcast, and become pumped up and ready to go. The next morning we say, "Now what?" Why? Our daily lives get in the way, and we fall into our regular routine. What was the reason for going to the seminar or listening to the podcast? It was to break out of the routine and pursue our passions. Doubt starts to creep in. We start thinking, "Who am I to think I can do something extraordinary? What I'm doing right now is safe and easy; things are good, so why should I try something new?" The bigger question is, What if you *don't* do it? You may be headed for a life of stagnation, complacency, being stuck in the same place, doing the same thing you already know you can do. Having doubts is normal, but once you

- have the burning desire and the interest, your *passion;*
- begin to take *action* by setting a goal and engaging your willpower and determination;
- *believe* in yourself and that you can do it;
- *focus* by setting aside time to work on your passionate pursuit;
- *simplify* your steps to get there by putting together a list, breaking the project down into manageable steps;
- *persist* by allowing nothing to get in the way of the time you set aside to do the work and pressing forward through setbacks; and
- *reflect* on the process and product of your work,

you will see accomplishment, and you will experience learning and growth. It may be the end result won't be exactly as you visualized it when you started, but by taking action on your passion and going through the step-by-step process, something will happen. You will have a different mindset, will have more confidence, and you will be encouraged by your ability to take action. This success will push you forward to try again, to

- *go for it,* a new venture, a new journey.

It will also be saved in your memory bank, a deposit in your emotional piggy bank as something for you to draw upon when obstacles come up. When I say obstacles, I mean challenges in the form of life events: an unexpected illness, a car accident, or an act of nature. It could be people questioning you on your pursuit, or doubt creeping in with your own mind, making things seems bigger than what they actually are. It happens to me, and I have options; I look around at my *Idea Poetry,* and I have my emotional savings piggy bank, my fuel, to make a withdrawal from to build me up when I need it.

Bringing the Steps to Life

To further bring these steps to life, let me tell you a story about a plan I made for one day in my life. I worked at Power 106 Radio in Los Angeles as a salesperson when it was a new radio station in the mid to late 1980s. The station switched format from easy listening music to a rap and hip hop station. Today, everybody knows what rap and hip hop music is and it's accepted. Back then, it was a new genre of music, and no other stations were playing it. Advertisers considered it to be the "gang banger station," meaning only gang members were listening, and they didn't see it as a viable option for advertising most products and services.

So here I was in Los Angeles, having moved from Milwaukee, selling a new radio station and being paid on 100 percent commission. I certainly wanted to be successful. I knew there was an audience listening beyond the perception of "just gang members." I even did research and found there were only sixty thousand gang members in the entire city. There were over one million listeners to the station, so there had to be more than just gang members listening! My challenge, my obstacle, was to convince advertisers of the value of the station and its listeners.

The audience was mostly young, male African Americans and Latinos. I was passionate about my work and wanted to be successful, and I wasn't going to let perceptions of others hold me back. I knew the strongest geographic area of the station's signal was in the inner city.

I took action by putting together a plan to make sales calls for one day in an urban area of the city on used car dealerships. There were ten to fifteen, and I could park my car and walk while making my sales calls.

I believed this was a good approach. Young, multicultural males lived in the area, and used cars were the perfect product for the station environment.

By focusing on one type of customer, I could use the same basic sales approach for each sales call.

I made a simple list and came up with twelve dealerships. I got the names of the general managers and owners, and I set out for the day.

Knocking on doors and making cold calls is hard work. Person after person turned me away; all were male business owners, either African American or Hispanic. I persisted, believing my plan was solid, and even if I heard no right now, I believed it didn't necessarily mean no forever. Maybe I would get a call two days later by leaving my business card. I kept at it. The end of the day was nearing, and I wouldn't say I had a lot of success. There was one more dealership on my list. I walked in, and something was different. I heard the radio station that I was selling blasting in the outdoor showroom. I looked around and saw shiny, used Mercedes Benzes, BMWs, Cadillacs, and various other car models. I decided to change my approach. I met with the owner and asked him why he was playing this music, because it wasn't typical for a car dealer showroom.

"The customers like it," he said. At that moment, he made the sale for me. He had no experience with radio advertising. We talked and started out with a small weekend campaign. It worked, and he quickly advertised at thirty thousand dollars per month for the next two years.

Reflecting on the process, was I lucky? I certainly was passionate about the work. I took action by putting together a plan and researching a geographic area and a product category that was a strategically good fit for the radio station. I believed enough to dedicate an entire day to my plan. I had my focus working for me by letting nothing get in the way of my day of sales calls, even though I knew it was going to be a tough day. I simplified the process by making a list and knowing exactly who I wanted to meet, and I persisted through the day even though nothing encouraging happened with the first eleven calls. I prepared myself for a successful day using my process, my step-by-step guide.

Upon reflection, I could see this was a good approach, and the success of making a sale gave me the energy to go for it, to begin again with other categories of business. Keep in mind, most of the *Idea Poetry* was not created at the time of this passionate pursuit. Many were created after as an expression of the current time. They're a reflection on my journeys, successes, and setbacks that have led me to realize my process.

As another example, I consistently watched the long-running reality television show, *American Idol.* Year after year I was inspired by the performances as well as the stories of the contestants.

As the field was narrowed to the top ten competitors more details of their journeys were highlighted. Most of the young people prepared for years before auditioning. Videos of them as kids standing in front of mirrors singing into hairbrushes for microphones were charming and humorous. Their stories were amazing portrayals of passion, burning desires to win the coveted prize, not only to fulfill their dreams of becoming singers, but to honor family and mentors who helped them on their passionate pursuit.

By the series finale I felt like I knew the finalists personally. I remember feeling their passion and watching as they took action by walking into the room for their first audition. Each person believing they had the talent and confidence to be the next American idol. I saw the focus they embodied to work and perform a new song week after week for the judges and viewers. As new challenges were given to the contestants they simplified the development of the next piece, letting go of the outcome of the previous week, and concentrating on the upcoming performance. The persistence through the process was amazing. They talked of exhaustion and sometimes conflict in direction they were given by the judges and mentors versus their own beliefs on the best approach to showcase their talent. Through it all they stuck with it, persisting. Each week the contestants were given feedback to reflect on to enhance their next performance. Every show they go for it, giving it all for the big prize, the realization of their dream.

My step by step process was used unconsciously! The final result was contestants transformed into performers. Imagine what you can accomplish by being aware of these steps to take to fulfill your worthy, passionate pursuits.

What Passions?

When we talk about passions, pursuits, and dreams, what are they? Your passion is very personal. It doesn't have to be something that changes the world. It should enhance your world, and that single element will serve to enrich the lives of others. You will become an inspiration to others by pursuing your dream. You will be a happier, more confident person knowing you are doing something with purpose.

What can your passion be? Honestly, it can be anything from starting a business to growing an existing business, to finding or maintaining a meaningful relationship. It can be teaching others about your passion or adopting a child and giving him a chance at a life he wouldn't have had if it weren't for you. What matters is that you have the passion to pursue it. This is about a process to set you up for success. All of us are in pursuit of something at all times. When we get it, it leads to something else. The joy, the happiness, is always in the pursuit.

The process presented in this writing works for short-term and long-term goals and pursuits. It works equally in your professional life and your personal life. You will find that these steps will become automatic; you don't have to carry around a checklist. With greater awareness, higher consciousness, and repetition, the magic and the success will appear.

As an example of how this can work in your personal life, I will tell you that whatever my work has been, it has always been my passion to the extent of obsession, even workaholism. I came to a realization at one point that something was missing, and something had to change. I wanted deeper, richer relationships in my life. Making that statement alone made it a passion, something I wanted to pursue.

It came to life by me taking action and setting a goal to make more time for my personal life, even if it was only on weekends to start. I believed the benefits of this action would make me a happier person, and my professional life would improve with time away from my work.

I put my focus on things of interest to me that involved interacting with other people. Beyond work, I always had a high activity level, however those were solo pursuits, running, working out on an elliptical, and more. By simplifying, I made a list and came up with things like writing, cooking, playing the piano, golf, and tennis. I researched options for all of these things. For a workaholic, this took persistence. Looking for ways to push myself out of my comfort zone and step out to learn new activities and meet new people as an adult was challenging.

By sticking with it, I found a writing group to explore my talents, and an opportunity to join a book club presented itself to me. I took piano and group golf and tennis lessons. The first time was difficult; however by showing up, I met other people in similar situations, and that made it easier to connect. This was some twenty years ago, and upon reflection I can say that it was a personally rewarding process and experience. The relationships formed from the book club are still intact and are probably the richest friendships I have ever had. The writing group led to other connections and encouraged me to write. I still play golf and am always meeting new people on the course. I continue to go for it, push myself out of my comfort zone and armed with my guide.

It's all about a process to help live inspired with commitment, purpose, and endless possibilities, which leads to a life of meaning. It's about the person you will become by identifying your passions and pursuing them.

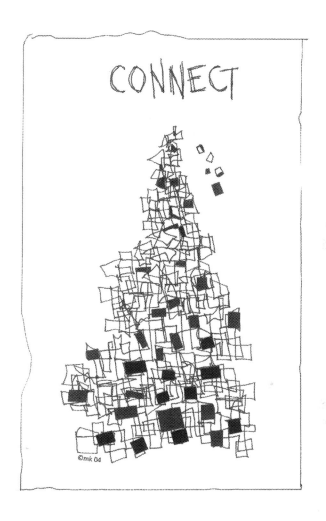

CONNECT

©mk 04

Let me give you another example of how my step-by-step guide was used. I was serving as a mentor to a young couple in passionate pursuit of a long-term personal goal. Having had a baby a few years ago, Liz and Rich were faced with unexpected expenses and acquired two loans with very high interest rates. After maturing and looking forward, they had a burning desire, a passion, to become debt free so they could save for the purchase of their first home.

Liz and Rich were successful in cleaning up all of their debt with the exception of the two high-interest loans. They took action

31

by setting a goal to attain a low-interest loan to pay off the two loans in full and have a reasonable payment on one consolidated loan. They believed all the work they had done to clean up their financial situation would help them. They focused their energies on living within a budget and sticking to the current payment plan. To simplify their process they made a list of financial institutions they already had relationships with to approach. They also made a list of professional and personal contacts that could help with referrals and references if necessary. Liz and Rich were prepared for whatever came up during potential inquiries.

One by one, they went down the list, and started making calls. Their current bank turned them down, as did other financial institutions. None would give them a loan, stating they had no credit and no assets. Liz and Rich persisted, believing their hard work of getting their finances in order and having a solid track record of paying on the existing loans made them worthy candidates.

Finally, a personal contact looked at their whole picture, including lifestyle and personal and professional goals. They received the low-interest loan, and it would be paid off in the next fifteen months with monthly payments 40 percent lower than their current payment.

Upon reflection, Liz and Rich said they learned a lot about finances. They saw if they were passionate about becoming debt free and then took action by setting a goal and believing they could do it, that was the start. The results would come by focusing their efforts on getting their finances in order, by simplifying the process by making a list of financial institutions and contacts, and by being persistent in the face of continual refusal.

As they make plans to go for it and begin their next adventure of saving for and purchasing their own home, Liz and Rich will be smarter and better equipped with their guide on how to pursue their passion.

How Do You Know What
Your Passion Is?

How do you know what your passion is? Finding one's passion is about really searching, taking the inner journey, and being conscious and aware of those moments of absorption, immersion, and flow, when time simply passes. I encourage you to ask yourself, "What am I doing when I am so absorbed that I lose track of time? What is that one thing I want to be known for? By applying the *Idea Poetry* steps, can I do it better than anyone else?"

Answering those questions requires introspection and deep thought. When you find the answers, you will notice there is some element of it, the passion, coming naturally and effortlessly. Even though there may be discomfort, the discomfort is where the magic happens, where the real work starts. I find comfort in the discomfort, trusting in my ability to believe, focus, and persist.

I find that to be true in putting together this presentation, in my yoga practice, in my work, and in my personal relationships. When things get difficult, I don't walk away; I stick with it and work through it, knowing enlightenment and a shift in perspective is coming.

With this writing, there were many times I felt it wasn't working, and I wanted to walk away. I literally walked away and went for a walk. I came back, and suddenly there it was: a new perspective.

How did I get here writing this book? I had a passion, an interest, and the burning desire to do something more. After years of creating my annual message, my *Idea Poetry*, I found encouragement from the recipients of these gifts. I would get responses like, "It's always great to get your holiday message, and once again you have inspired me." In 2004 I launched a website that displays the designs and offers the opportunity for people to send inspiring e-cards for free, and to buy note cards, mini cards, or framed desktop prints. Now I wanted to take it a step further and create this book in order to have opportunities to present the ideas as a narrative or workshop. My next adventure begins.

I took action by setting a goal, a commitment, and by engaging my willpower and determination. It became a priority in my life, and I took steps to move toward it by writing and, doing the actual work. I believed that I had something unique to offer, and I focused by making time every day to work on it. I simplified the process with an outline of what should be included, and I consistently persisted at it over the last six months by not letting anything get in the way of my writing time. With continual reflection, I am here with you, right now, sharing my passion!

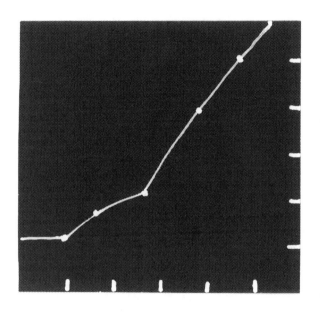

BELIEVE
ENCOURAGE
INSPIRE
WATCH!

©MK 04

My Challenges

Whatever I do, from making a presentation, publishing my ideas, or creating and sharing a new design, I still have fears and doubts, and that's part of it for me. How am I going to do it? Will it be good enough? Will it reach people? "It has in the past, and it will again," I say to myself. It will be good enough for those who were meant to see it, hear my presentation, read it, and be touched by it.

What's at stake for me if I don't pursue my passion? I'd be relegated to a life of saying *what if,* and I'd take the safe route of doing things I know I can do. Being brave enough to try something new is a virtue, a chance for growth. If I'm not moving forward in this life, I'm moving backward. It's my obligation to give back the gift I was given for communicating simple, timeless, meaningful messages to inspire and motivate. I have to give life to this passion and leave it behind as my legacy, just as you have to give life to yours.

Letting Go of Fear and Ego

Fear and ego play a role in holding us back from pursuing our passion. I have had my fears of putting my work out there: What if you pay for this book and then devote some of your valuable time to read it, and it doesn't move you at all? What if you're not inspired or enlightened, and you get nothing out of it? That was a fear that held me back.

I have had excuses to not do it: I don't have time. I'm too busy. I have to walk my dog. I have to brush my teeth. I have to work. I have to work out. I have to pay bills. I have to sleep. I have to relax, because I've worked all week. All that is true, and I do those things, but then the days turn into weeks, the weeks turn into months, the months turn into years, and I'm still feeling that longing, that yearning for something more.

While doing all the things I have to do, I can justify that if I don't take that step and do the thing that brings joy, I never have to deal with the fear of *what if*. What if it doesn't work out for me? What if I concentrate on this thing that makes me forget about time because I'm so absorbed, so inspired, so in spirit—and it doesn't work? I fail. I don't achieve. I don't reach my desired outcome. How will I feel? And what about my ego, that mediator between the person and reality? Well, it's about reaching that place where the ego doesn't matter; the achievement isn't important, and the reality of complacency is worse than any fear I could have. It's about doing what will bring me peace and add meaning to my life.

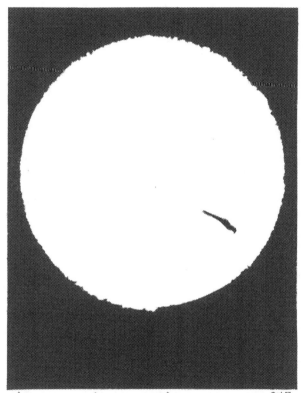

©mk 87

there's always time

The Rewards

That passion, that drive, that burning desire—we all have it for something. It has be nurtured, cultivated, and realized, or else we'll never feel that feeling, that exhilaration for life that makes our senses astute and alive from the top of our heads to the soles of our feet.

We begin to notice everyday things that cause us to pause and appreciate the moment. I have a lemon tree in my backyard. Before the blossoms turn to little balls of green that eventually become lemons, the hummingbirds hang in midair with their long beaks attached to the blossoms, and they make that humming sound. I know many times I have missed that moment because I'm not as present. The more I do my own work and follow my heart, the more aware I am of the precious moments in life that cause me to stop and notice the wonder all around me, the wonder that is my life. That's real living, and I want that.

HEART
HAS
SOUL

Synchronicity: Paying Attention to the Signs

What happens along the way? I find when I set a goal for myself and am committed and in pursuit of something I'm passionate about, I start noticing things. Magazine articles, email blasts, and radio and television shows give me ideas and encouragement to move forward. You might think it's coincidence, but it's synchronicity, alignment: when I decide to do something, the universe steps in and sends me signs to let me know I'm on the right path.

I have talked about giving life to my designs for years not only with my website, but by sharing my story in writing and through live presentations, just like I'm doing now.

When I finally committed to it, I received an e-mail from a woman who facilitates workshops for people to write and tell their personal stories. I took the workshop; put together the narrative called *Beyond Fear and Ego*, and then followed up by writing this book. I know I received e-mails about that workshop before, but I didn't notice them. So why on that day did I notice it? Because I'd made the commitment to take action on my passion and set it as a goal, and it came into my life at precisely the right moment. The universe was offering me support and letting me know this was the right time. Synchronicity!

Everything I need and want will come to me at the right moment. The things I focus on will come to me. We get what we focus on.

Where Does the Inspiration Come From?

The best answer I can give you is everywhere. I devour my surroundings and my environment. I make connections between things unrelated to each other. When struggling in a yoga pose, I liken it to a difficult conversation in my personal or work life. I breathe through the yoga pose and do the same in life. I stay with it, knowing I will get through it with passion, positive actions, belief, focus, simplifying the issues and tasks, consistently persisting, and reflecting.

I listen to people in real time, on TV, and on the radio. I take notes. I use all of my senses to notice things, write stuff down, date it, analyze it, and study it. I never know when I will use it, but eventually I will.

Let me tell you about the FOCUS design, how it came about, and the action and synchronicity that took place to create it. The hardest step in any endeavor is the first step, beginning.

If you're a writer, you have to consistently return to your desk and write; if you're a teacher, you have to do your preparation before the students step into the classroom. As a farmer, you have to plant seeds and water. That blank piece of paper, that empty field in front of you is the scariest thing in the world.

When I started to create a new piece of *Idea Poetry*, sometimes it would come easy and sometimes it wouldn't. I would start doodling so there would be something on the page. I will never forget how one time my cat came in the room after digging in a houseplant. She jumped up on the desk and walked all over my drawing pad, leaving paw prints of mud all over the page. I started to brush away the dirt, and what was left was quite unique: these little wispy hair imprints from her paws that I could have never drawn on my own.

It was a start; it was the universe stepping in to give me a start. I no longer had a blank piece of paper, and it was the inspiration to create the FOCUS design.

Let's Try the Process with an Exercise

Passion: The Adventure Begins with You

What are you doing when you are so absorbed that you lose track of time?

_____

_____

_____

_____

_____

_____

What is your unique talent, something that you do better than anyone else?

_____

_____

_____

_____

_____

_____

What do you want to be known for?

_____

_____

_____

_____

_____

_____

Based on the above, are there some things you are interested in and have a burning desire to pursue? They can be short term or long term, personal or professional. List them. If you already have a passion you want to pursue, list that as well.

_____

_____

_____

_____

_____

_____

Action: Nothing Happens Until Something Moves

Choose something you are willing to commit to, something worthy of a passionate pursuit. Write it down.

_____

_____

_____

_____

_____

_____

How can you begin to take action? Can you set a goal? Can you share it with another person to create accountability?

_____

_____

_____

_____

_____

_____

What else will help you begin pursuit of your passion?

_____

_____

_____

_____

_____

_____

Believe: I believe in you. Do you?

Do you believe you have the capabilities to pursue your passion physically, intellectually, and passionately? If not, what is holding you back?

_____

_____

_____

_____

_____

What will help you bolster the belief in your passionate pursuit?

_____

_____

_____

_____

_____

_____

Focus: We Get What We Focus On

Is it enough of a priority in your life to dedicate a concentrated effort and time to the necessary work? If so, what does your schedule allow for?

_____

_____

_____

_____

_____

_____

Is it something that you can own, that you can put your unique stamp on and have it be identified as uniquely yours? If so, how?

_____

_____

_____

_____

_____

_____

If not, what steps can you take to make it a priority and something you can own?

_____

_____

_____

_____

_____

_____

Simplify: Step by step so it doesn't seem so daunting!

Make a list. Break your project into manageable steps that you can check off, so you can feel accomplished and know what to do next.

Persist: Consistently persisting is everything!

Can you consistently persist on your pursuit, not giving up when obstacles present themselves? If yes, list examples of when you have demonstrated your determination in previous challenging situations. (It's something to draw upon to remind yourself you have done it before.)

Are you willing to keep trying, making adjustments as necessary to see your pursuit through to completion? If yes, write it down, make the commitment to yourself, and set a deadline for milestones and completion.

If not, what can you do to engage your ability to be consistently persistent?

_____

_____

_____

_____

_____

_____

Reflect: Continual reflection during and after the process is necessary for a positive experience and future growth.

Have you ever worked on a project where, during the process, you or a team felt it wasn't working, and you made a significant change in direction? If so, describe what happened.

_____

_____

_____

_____

_____

_____

How did that help the process and the end result?

_____

_____

_____

_____

_____

_____

Based on the above experience, would you do anything differently when starting a new project or pursuit?

_____

_____

_____

_____

_____

Reflect during and after completion of a passionate pursuit. Ask, "What worked? What didn't work? What can be improved upon?"

_____

_____

_____

_____

_____

Go For It!

It's time to begin a passionate pursuit or enhance something you have already done. Record your steps and progress.

Good luck!

Passion

_____
_____
_____
_____
_____
_____

Action

_____
_____
_____
_____
_____
_____

Believe

_____
_____
_____
_____
_____
_____

Focus

_____
_____
_____
_____
_____
_____

Simplify

_____

_____

_____

_____

_____

Persist

_____

_____

_____

_____

_____

Reflect

_____

_____

_____

_____

_____

Bonus Tips

- Deadlines encourage progress. Create deadlines for yourself if there are no external ones imposed by others.
- Tell people close to you about what you're working on. Create accountability so they ask you about it. Surely you will want to have updates when asked.
- When you feel you're finished for the day, do one more task to move forward. Over the course of a year, that's 365 more things done!
- Look at your project or goal before finishing for the day; leave something unfinished so you immediately have a place to start the next day. No saying, "Now what?" It will make you excited to finish what you started the day before.
- Think for days and sleep with your project or goal. Let it incubate and roll around in your head. You'll be amazed at how much you get done in just one hour. Let the energy build.
- Make it yours. Own it. With anything you do, make sure you put your unique stamp on it. That thing that makes it uniquely yours by using your distinct skills and experiences.
- Reward yourself. Plan to stop working at a set time or once a milestone is reached, and then do something that's fun for you before getting back to it. You deserve it.
- Watch sports for inspiration. Every point, every play is executed with heart, soul, and passion. The next play, it starts all over. There's no dwelling on the past, good or bad; the athlete shakes it off and is in the now. Do that!
- Have a successful attitude, a successful consciousness. Assume everything is stacked in your favor, and be grateful for it. It will become a reality.
- Use the ripple effect. Ride the wave, because one successful project leads to another. Expect it and keep it going.

THERE'S NOTHING
ORDINARY ABOUT...

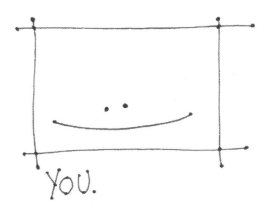

YOU.

GO MAKE THE DAY HAPPEN!
©MK95

All *Idea Poetry* Designs

Idea Poetry can be used in every aspect of life. Choose individual designs that speak to you, or group them together to create your own step-by-step guide. In your work life, you can use them to advance your career, get that dream job, or have a guide to put together a presentation or a plan for a day's work. They can be used in personal situations to enhance relationships with family, friends, and colleagues.

To demonstrate how idea poetry designs can be used to guide additional paths I have outlined two other groupings beyond the pursuit of passion presented earlier.

The programs can be implemented by sending e-cards from my website or giving cards or mini cards, or by simply practicing the concepts with words and actions.

1. New Team Member Welcome

Empower a new team member by letting him know:

- it's the *people* that make companies succeed;
- you were brought into the group to contribute and *be who you are;*
- *connect* with other team members for ongoing growth and success;
- *be bold and take risks* with respect for the company, its values, and other team members;
- *if a door closes, a new one opens;* if
- you *persist;* and remember that
- tomorrow offers a *new beginning.*

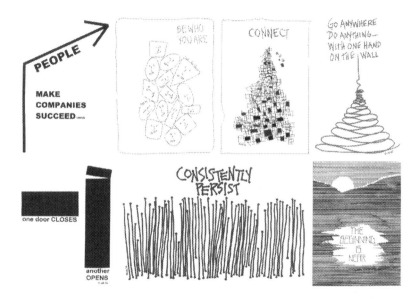

PEOPLE

**MAKE
COMPANIES
SUCCEED**

BE WHO YOU ARE

CONNECT

GO ANYWHERE
DO ANYTHING—
WITH ONE HAND
ON THE WALL

one door CLOSES

another OPENS

CONSISTENTLY PERSIST

THE BEGINNING IS NEAR

2. Inspiration to Lift Someone's Spirit

A friend or family member is feeling down and uninspired, let her know:

- you're *glad she was born;*
- *life* can be *complicated and sweet* at the same time;
- remember to *live; love, laugh* through it all; and
- *wishes* help for those low moments; and always
- be *grateful for and appreciate* those that keep your spirit alive.

I'M GLAD
YOU
WERE
BORN

COMPLICATED
INTRICATE
SWEET

LIFE

Live Love Laugh
Look Learn

WISHES

SOMETHING
To Do
To Love
To Hope For

©nk 04

To do:
Prepare for meetings
check e-mail
answer e-mails (all of them)
analyze sales
reproject budget
wash car
meet with everyone
write recap of meetings
return phone calls

appreciate those that
keep my spirit alive!
(every day).

©nk 01

Additionally, I have used my step-by-step guide, Seven Steps to Pursue Your Passions, Plus One, when practicing yoga, working on a difficult pose, and improving my golf game. The activities require passion, action, belief in oneself, focus, simplifying the steps, persistence, and reflection. I don't step on my yoga mat, walk the golf course, or enter into any passionate pursuit without my guide.

Look at all *Idea Poetry* designs and choose what speaks to you at any given time on your journey.

The Beginning Is Near

A constant source of inspiration.
Nothing comes to an end; rather, something is always beginning.
A new day.
A new project.
Another chance to pursue my dreams and passions.
What is beginning for you?

Nothing Ordinary

Find ways to differentiate yourself from others.
Make it yours;
bring your uniqueness to everything you do.
This is the high achiever in each of us.
Look at it before taking a conference call,
before leaving the office for a day of visiting clients,
or as the team mom heading for the big soccer game.
How can you own it?

THERE'S NOTHING ORDINARY ABOUT...

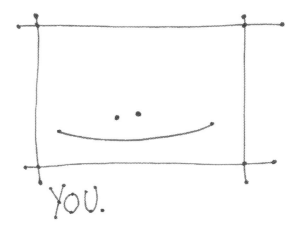

YOU.

GO MAKE THE DAY HAPPEN!

©MK95

Searching

We're all searching for answers
for one thing or one person to make us happy and fulfilled.
The answer for all of us lies in our own hearts.
Remind yourself of it every day,
and discover the power of taking control of your own destiny by
looking within.

Searching——

©mk 04

Look within

Wishes

I wish for you something rewarding to do in life,
Something you want to do so much that time passes without being
conscious of it.
I wish for you something or someone to love,
And something to hope for to make every day exhilarating, joyous,
and inspiring.

Connect

Discover the magic of getting connected.
Be inspired by the benefits of surrounding yourself with other talented people who can
enhance your ability to succeed in your personal and professional pursuits.
Realize your connection to others.
Reach out, connect, and watch your triumphs and theirs soar.

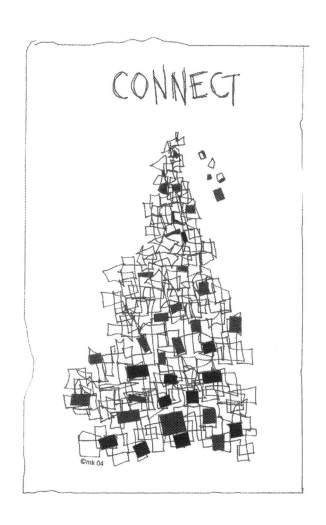

CONNECT

©mk 04

Focus

All of us have so much information coming at us every day.
It is our job to cut through the clutter, focus on one task one feeling
at a time, and see it through to completion before beginning the
next.
Nothing can take the place of a focused, concentrated effort.
You get what you focus on.
What will you get?

Nothing Happens

Take action.
Nothing happens, until something moves and I take that first action step.
Set a goal, make a commitment of the will, and move toward the goal.
If I do nothing, nothing happens.
Begin.

NOTHING HAPPENS

© MK 06

UNTIL
SOMETHING
MOVE S

Plan

All great triumphs begin as a wish, a dream;
then the burning desire, the passion;
then the action, the plan to make it happen.
Move your wishes and dreams forward, and take the action step.

IT

TAKES

AS

MUCH

EFFORT

TO

WISH

AS

IT

DOES

TO

PLAN © MK 06

PLAN
TO
DOES
IT
AS
WISH
TO
EFFORT
MUCH
AS
TAKES
IT

Simplify

Remind yourself to simplify every day,
and be inspired by the time and space you create.
Starting a new project always seems overwhelming.
Break it down into manageable steps, chunks, so it doesn't seem so
daunting.
Write them down.
Check the list.
I pick up where I left off.
It's old school.
It works.

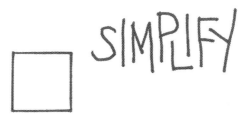 SIMPLIFY

Passion and Adventure

The adventure is our passion.
Passion is interest plus a burning desire.
Discover your passion by noticing those moments of flow, of absorption,
when time passes as you are involved in work that is uniquely yours.
This is the foundation of the process, and it begins personally with
me, with you.
Go there.

The Adventure
Begins...

With You.

©mk 04

Companies Succeed

Companies succeed because of great people.
Let people in your company know they own the success of the company.

Good, Better, Best

A personal mantra for everyone.
Remind yourself every day.

DON'T STOP UNTIL YOUR GOOD IS BETTER AND YOUR BETTER IS BEST

GOOD

DON'T STOP UNTIL YOUR GOOD IS BETTER AND YOUR BETTER IS BEST

BETTER

DON'T STOP UNTIL YOUR GOOD IS BETTER AND YOUR BETTER IS BEST

BEST

DON'T STOP UNTIL YOUR GOOD IS BETTER AND YOUR BETTER IS BEST
DON'T STOP UNTIL YOUR GOOD IS BETTER AND YOUR BETTER IS BEST
DON'T STOP UNTIL YOUR GOOD IS BETTER AND YOUR BETTER IS BEST
DON'T STOP UNTIL YOUR GOOD IS BETTER AND YOUR BETTER IS BEST
DON'T STOP UNTIL YOUR GOOD IS BETTER AND YOUR BETTER IS BEST
DON'T STOP UNTIL YOUR GOOD IS BETTER AND YOUR BETTER IS BEST
DON'T STOP UNTIL YOUR GOOD IS BETTER AND YOUR BETTER IS BEST
DON'T STOP UNTIL YOUR GOOD IS BETTER AND YOUR BETTER IS BEST
DON'T STOP UNTIL YOUR GOOD IS BETTER AND YOUR BETTER IS BEST
DON'T STOP UNTIL YOUR GOOD IS BETTER AND YOUR BETTER IS BEST
DON'T STOP UNTIL YOUR GOOD IS BETTER AND YOUR BETTER IS BEST
DON'T STOP UNTIL YOUR GOOD IS BETTER AND YOUR BETTER IS BEST
DON'T STOP UNTIL YOUR GOOD IS BETTER AND YOUR BETTER IS BEST

©mk06

One Door

Adversities are part of everyone's life.
Nature does not allow something of value to be taken away without replacing it with something of equal or greater value.
Look for the open door in every setback.
Be hopeful and inspired by the new opportunities that will surely present themselves.

one door CLOSES

another
OPENS
© mk 04

Persist

Some people say attitude is everything; I say attitude is *almost* everything.
Persistence, sticking with it consistently, is everything.
Obstacles will show up—life events, negative comments from others,
one's own mind creating problems, doubt, and worry.
It will happen to you too.
Stay the course, and you will succeed beyond expectations.

CONSISTENTLY
PERSIST

Believe

If I believe I can do something, I can do it. I will do it.
Take action and believe in what you are doing.
Believe it from your heart.
Little steps come together to make the whole.
I believe in you.

©mk 95

People

If you lead a company of one, one hundred, or more,
let your people know they make the difference.

PEOPLE

MAKE
COMPANIES
SUCCEED ©MK06

Incandescent

Plug into your uniqueness.
Find the bright spot in your life every day, in everything and everyone.

LET YOUR'S BE INCANDESCENT

LIFE TODAY

© Mk 91

99

You Deserve It

Take a break from the routine and rigors of the day.
You deserve it,
and you'll be back with a fresh perspective.

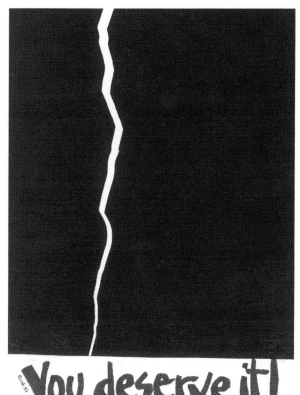

You deserve it!

Glad You Were Born

Let people know today how happy you are to have them in your life. Watch your relationships soar.

Begin It Now

I am constantly inspired to get started today,
to make my dreams a reality.
Begin now, again and again.

LIFE...
begin it now,
again.

Heart Has Soul

When I bring my heart, my passion, into whatever I'm doing, that's when things happen.
It's the part of me that believes, trusts, and knows intuitively that I can do it,
even if my head says no.
Lead with your heart, and your head and hands will follow.

HEART
HAS
SOUL

With Every Birth

Excitement, energy, and rebirth come from a new job.
Promotion, new relationship, birth of a child, new home purchase, etc.
All of the wonderful experiences life has to offer us every day!
What meaning does it have for you?

Be For Each Other

Imagine a single ring floating in space.
No team, partnership, or family can survive
without the realization that we are all connected and are integral
parts of a whole.
We are all in it together.
Be for each other.

be for
each other.
© MK96

Holiday

Every day is a holiday to celebrate you,
your life,
who you are,
and who you are becoming
in pursuit of your passions.

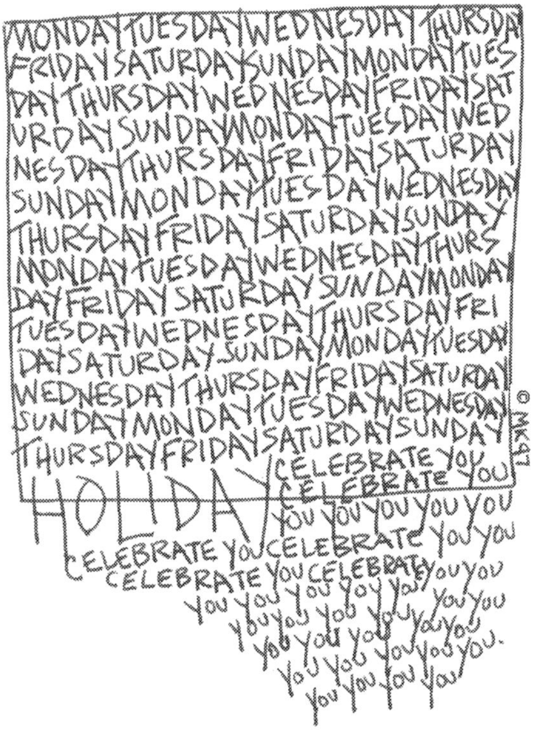
MONDAY TUESDAY WEDNESDAY THURSDA
FRIDAY SATURDAY SUNDAY MONDAY TUES
DAY THURSDAY WEDNESDAY FRIDAY SAT
URDAY SUNDAY MONDAY TUESDAY WED
NESDAY THURSDAY FRIDAY SATURDAY
SUNDAY MONDAY TUESDAY WEDNESDAY
THURSDAY FRIDAY SATURDAY SUNDAY
MONDAY TUESDAY WEDNESDAY THURS
DAY FRIDAY SATURDAY SUNDAY MONDAY
TUESDAY WEDNESDAY THURSDAY FRI
DAY SATURDAY SUNDAY MONDAY TUESDAY
WEDNESDAY THURSDAY FRIDAY SATURDAY
SUNDAY MONDAY TUESDAY WEDNESDAY
THURSDAY FRIDAY SATURDAY SUNDAY
HOLIDAY CELEBRATE YOU CELEBRATE YOU
YOU YOU YOU YOU YOU
CELEBRATE YOU CELEBRATE YOU YOU
CELEBRATE YOU CELEBRATE YOU YOU
YOU.
© MK97

Live, Love, Laugh

Live, Love, Laugh, Look, Learn
Do all of these
every day
and as often as possible!

Live Love Laugh
Look Learn

To Do List

Back to basics with a to do list.
It should be part of everyone's life at home and work.
One item should never be crossed off the list
and should always be carried over for tomorrow.
Do you remember every day?

To do:

~~Prepare for meetings~~
~~check e-mail~~
~~answer e-mails~~ (all of them)
~~analyze sales~~
~~reproject budget~~
~~wash car~~
~~meet with everyone~~
~~write recap of meetings~~
~~return phone calls~~

appreciate those that
keep my spirit alive!
(every day).

©mk 01

Life

Choose your attitude toward life.
Is it difficult?
Full of setbacks and disappointments?
Or is this complex web we call life complicated, intricate, and sweet,
to be savored and enjoyed?
What will your attitude be today?

COMPLICATED
INTRICATE
SWEET

LIFE

Es Lo Que Es (It Is What It Is)

No matter what happens,
it simply is what it is.
Find the opportunity in everything.

Be Who You Are

Your gifts, skills, and talents are unique,
and are not to be wasted trying to be like someone else.
It's the ultimate compliment and show of acceptance
to encourage yourself and others to "be who you are."
Be inspired by the wonderful you.

There's Always Time

There's always time
for the important things.
Take time to pursue your passion,
that which leads you to a life of personal fulfillment.

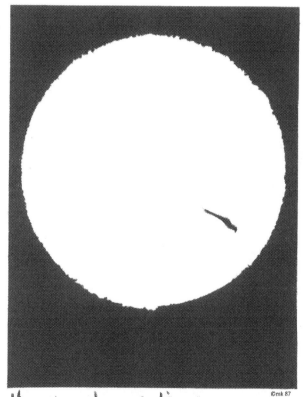

there's always time

©mk 87

Go Anywhere

Discover a sense of hope and encouragement.
Don't let go of your dreams.
The single, continuous line represents the journey.
Navigate your wonderful life with one hand on the wall of life's maze.
You will never be lost.

No Accidents

Everything happens for a reason.
Everything comes into your life at precisely the right moment,
when you are ready to receive it.
Notice it.
Cherish it.
Be grateful for it, whatever the moment brings.

THERE ARE
NO ACCIDENTS!

LIVE EVERY
    MOMENT.
©mk 01

Go For It

Why not?
Do everything bold
and in your own unique style.
Start a new project, or improve and enhance what was just completed.
It's never over!

GO
FOR
IT

© MK 90

Watch!

We're all team leaders of some kind—
parents, managers, athletic coaches, business executives.
Discover the power of
believing,
encouraging,
and inspiring,
and watch the results!

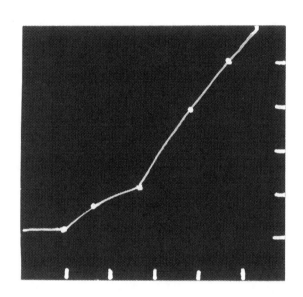

BELIEVE
ENCOURAGE
INSPIRE
WATCH!

©MK 04

youdeservethismoment.com

It's okay to turn off the computer, TV, or cell phone
and just be,
for however long it takes to refresh you.

OFF

Reflect

Let ideas and thoughts incubate.
Allow your mind and body the necessary time to rejuvenate
and reassess your goals, actions, and triumphs.
What worked?
What didn't work?
What could be better?
Continual reflection produces the best possible result and inspiration
to move forward.

Big Hug

Big hug
to you.

My Hope for You

What do I want for you? What do I hope for you? I hope you will not just want a job and a place to go every day, but a life filled with passion, purpose, and possibilities. I hope you will release your fears, take action, let go of your ego, forget about achievement, and do what makes you happy. I hope you'll try my step-by-step guide and find you will never be at a loss for what to do next. I hope you realize we're all significant, and it's up to each one of us to find our significance in our own way.

There is no one who has your exact set of skills and experiences to make the work you're doing uniquely yours. I hope that you will take a little piece of my message, and that the essence of what I'm doing inspires you on your personal journey.

This journey called life is about the person you become along the way while pursuing your passions.

LIFE...
begin it now,
again.

About the Author

Marie Kordus has a degree in Fine Arts from Cardinal Stritch University in Milwaukee, WI. She moved to Los Angeles, where she currently resides, to pursue work as an art director for films, and later, she co-owned a talent agency. Her skills and interests eventually attracted her to broadcasting and media, where she excelled. Marie has an extensive background in the broadcast industry, including senior management positions in both radio and television sales and marketing.

Combining her business experience with her artistic talent Marie is the founder of HiBrowsing.com where her inspirational designs to inspire and motivate people to their highest calling are displayed.

Marie wrote and performed a one-person show on the pursuit of passion, Beyond Fear and Ego. She also co-authored a book, Stepping Stones to Success, with celebrity authors, Deepak Chopra and Jack Canfield, offered as an e-book.

Marie is available to speak and teach workshops using the concepts in this book.

Website: www.hibrowsing.com

Printed in the United States
By Bookmasters